■SCHOLAST

Riddle Poem of the Day

180 Delightful, Guess-Me Poems That Build Early Reading and Listening Skills—All Year Long!

by Betsy Franco

New York • Toronto • London • Auckland • Sydney
Mexico City • New Delhi • Hong Kong • Buenos Aires

Teaching *Resources*

For Andrew

Cover design by Anna Christian
Cover and interior artwork by Rusty Fletcher
Interior design by Solutions by Design, Inc.

ISBN: 0-439-51384-7

1 2 3 4 5 6 7 8 9 10   40   14 13 12 11 10 09 08 07 06 05

Contents

February

March

April

May

June

Riddles wake up children's minds in so many ways! They're fun to read and they're fun to guess. And they can enrich every part of the curriculum and school day.

Riddle Poem of the Day offers the luxury of having a lively riddle at your fingertips every day of the school year. Riddles are grouped by month—and the themes most prominent in each month—from September to June. Each month provides you with more than a dozen riddles, including an open-ended riddle children can complete themselves.

Riddles have many built-in benefits. They . . .

- ◎ sharpen critical thinking skills.
- ◎ promote oral literacy.
- ◎ teach word families, phonics, and rhyming skills.
- ◎ introduce and reinforce themes in all areas of the curriculum.
- ◎ encourage creativity.

BUILDING SKILLS WITH THE RIDDLE POEMS

The riddle poems in *Riddle Poem of the Day* are written for a variety of settings and situations. Here are a few ideas for putting riddle poems to work in the classroom.

Sharpening Critical Thinking Skills

Every riddle is an opportunity to build critical thinking skills. In its basic form, a riddle is a set of clues. Using logical reasoning, children put the clues together to find the answer. They learn new information and apply problem-solving strategies. When introducing and reading a riddle, ask questions such as:

- ◎ Do you think the answer is a person, place or thing? Why?
- ◎ Who thinks they might know the answer after hearing this clue?
- ◎ How did you figure out the answer?

Promoting Oral Literacy

Reproducing a riddle on a pocket chart or on an overhead will enable the whole class to participate at once, especially during circle time or shared reading.

These riddles are ideal for developing oral literacy in young learners. You can read the riddle aloud as children read along. Then students can read the riddle individually or with a partner, in front of the class. Riddles can even become poems for two voices as two groups take turns reading every other line:

> It's a soft, dark home for roots to grow.
> **It's where I plant my seeds.**
> I keep it nice and wet.
> **I dig out all its weeds.**
> What does my garden need? _____

Riddles work well in literacy centers, too. Children can read, copy, and illustrate the riddle. And, of course, they can write the answer!

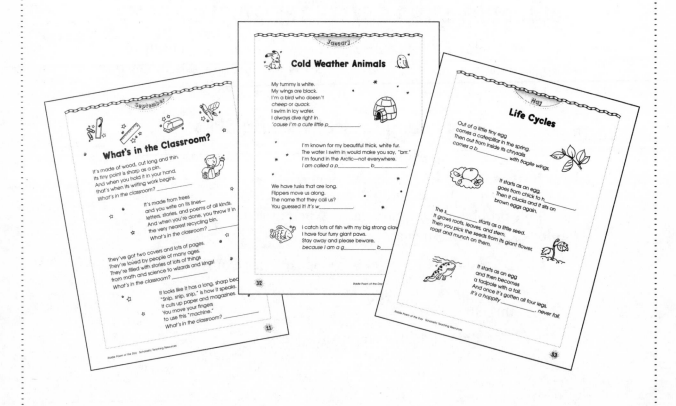

Teaching Word Families, Phonics, and Rhyming

The riddles in this book are told in rhymed verse. Children might circle the rhyming words. They can then list other words in that word family.

In some cases, the answer to the riddle *is* the final rhyming word. Children will have fun brainstorming the possible answers:

> Raw or cooked
> or part of soup,
> There are many ways to prepare it.
> It's orange with wild green leaves on top.
> *It's a crunchy, munchy _____.*

Some riddles have alliteration (in which a beginning consonant is repeated). In some cases, the first letter of the answer is given. This provides an opportunity to stress beginning consonants:

> I'm waiting inside
> all **f**uzzy and yellow.
> I have **f**eathers and wings.
> I'm a cute little **f**ellow.
> *Who's inside the egg? _____*

> On Thanksgiving day,
> no matter the weather,
> the people you love
> all gather together . . .
> *as a f_____.*

Riddles can be used to emphasize a phonemic element. Call attention to words with a particular sound, such as short *i* and long *i*:

> **I'm** up in the **sky**
> on a clear, **bright night**.
> **I twinkle**. **I wink**.
> **I'm** a sparkly **light**.
> *I'm a _____.*

When answers come in related sets, such as days of the week, you can write the answers on cards. Students can analyze the similarities and differences among the words on the cards.

Introducing and Reinforcing Themes in the Curriculum

In each section, the riddles are divided into themes, with four or five riddles per topic. Some touch on a social studies topic, such as community helpers or transportation:

> I spy with my little eye
> someone checking the beat of my heart.
> She looks in my mouth to check my throat.
> Then she writes things down on her little chart.
> *I spy a _____.*

In some months, the riddles introduce a science topic, such as space or life cycles:

> Out of a little tiny egg
> comes a caterpillar in the spring.
> Then out from inside its chrysalis
> *comes a b_____ with fragile wings.*

Throughout, math concepts are included in both traditional and open-ended bonus riddles, giving children a chance to practice their math learning over and over again.

> ____ little chimps
> were swinging in a tree.
> ____ more came
> and hung by their knees.
> That is _____ chimps in all,
> as silly as can be—
> swinging and hanging
> from the jungle tree.

Encouraging Creativity

Have children illustrate their answers. Or, have some children act out the riddle while others read it aloud.

These riddles can help you from the start of the day until those final minutes before the bell rings. They have so many uses and so many benefits. Students will find them fun and fresh, *every day, all year round!*

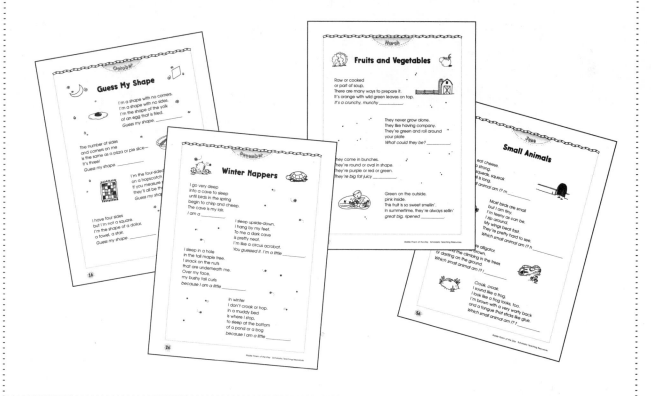

Write Your Own Riddles

For extra fun, you'll find riddle frames throughout the book (pages 15, 20, 25, 30, 35, 40, 45, 50, 55, and 60). Children can write their very own riddles and have a friend (or the whole group) guess the answer. Simply copy the frames onto chart paper (or reproduce them on an overhead), and invite children to complete them. You might try writing the riddle together as a group first, to demonstrate how it's done.

What's in the Classroom?

It's made of wood, cut long and thin.
Its tiny point is sharp as a pin.
And when you hold it in your hand,
that's when its writing work begins.
What's in the classroom? _____

It's made from trees
and you write on its lines—
letters, stories, and poems of all kinds.
And when you're done, you can throw it in
the very nearest recycling bin.
What's in the classroom? _____

They've got two covers and lots of pages.
They're loved by people of many ages.
They're filled with stories of lots of things,
from math and science to wizards and kings!
What's in the classroom? _____

It looks like it has a long, sharp beak.
"Snip, snip, snip," is how it speaks.
It cuts up paper and magazines.
You move your fingers
to use this "machine."
What's in the classroom? _____

Feelings

When something's unfair,
sparks seem to fly
right out of the top of my head.
I feel like yelling and stomping around
and my cheeks turn very red,
When I feel _____.

If my dog is hurt
or a good friend moves,
my smile is a frown.
I've got the blues,
When I feel _____.

When I get this bright yellow feeling,
I want to dance and cheer.
I feel like jumping up and down
and I grin from ear to ear,
When I feel _____.

I'd paint this feeling in orange and black
'cause it's fun to feel it on Halloween.
A haunted house makes goose bumps come
when it's dark in there and I want to scream,
When I feel _____.

Riddle Poem of the Day Scholastic Teaching Resources

Which School Subject?

How many bugs left in the tree?
What is 3 plus 3 plus 3?
We count along the number line path.
We add, subtract, and measure in _____.

Books can take us to outer space
and they let us meet people from every place.
As we head for the shelves, we feel like stampeding
when our teacher says it's time for _____.

We sprinkle glitter to look like snow.
We paint some masks to make them glow.
We make a dragon and color each part
as we paint and cut and paste in _____.

How does a tadpole change to a frog?
What things float? What makes fog?
We learn so much, our brains must be giants
when we experiment in _____.

Which Day of the Week?

I always start the school week,
I'm very proud to say.
I start with *M* like *monkey* does.
I'm quite a special day.
Which day am I? _____

I'm the very last one
of the school days.
I come just before the weekend
when there's lots of time to play!
Which day am I? _____

My name begins like *thirsty*
and *thirty* and *thumb* and *third*.
Wednesday comes before me
and Friday's afterward.
Which day am I? _____

Riddle Poem of the Day Scholastic Teaching Resources

I'm in the middle of every week.
I start with a *W*.
I always come after Tuesday's done.
That's what I like to do.
Which day am I? _____

When you say the days of the school week,
I'm always the second day.
Whenever children say my name,
the number "two" is what they say.
Which day am I? _____

Write Your Own Riddle:
Guess Which Student

This student has hair
that's the color _____
                    (Fill in the color.)
and two _____ eyes to see.
            (Fill in the color.)
This student likes to _____ and _____.
                        (Fill in favorite sports or activities.)
Now guess who it could be! _____

Guess My Shape

I'm a shape with no corners.
I'm a shape with no sides.
I'm the shape of the yolk
of an egg that is fried.
Guess my shape. _____

The number of sides
and corners on me
is the same as a pizza or pie slice—
it's three!
Guess my shape. _____

I'm the four-sided shape
on a hopscotch game.
If you measure my sides,
they'll all be the same.
Guess my shape. _____

I have four sides
but I'm not a square.
I'm the shape of a dollar,
a towel, a stair.
Guess my shape. _____

Riddle Poem of the Day Scholastic Teaching Resources

Fall Things

It whistles and whooshes.
It swishes and blows.
It twirls fall leaves
wherever it goes.
What is it? _____

They grow in the fall,
they're picked from a tree.
Crunch. Crunch. Take a bite
of yellow, red, or green.
What are they? _____

Their color is a bright, bright orange.
Their leaves are big and green.
They grow and grow so round and plump
They wait for Halloween.
What are they? _____

In fall, they put on a color show.
They change their colors before the snow.
Red, orange, yellow, brown,
They all let go
and fall to the ground.
What are they? _____

Halloween

In the night, it flies around.
In the day, it's upside down.
With fur on its body
and big, wide wings,
It's one of the coolest Halloween things.
This Halloween animal is a _____.

Carve a silly or scary face
after taking out the seeds.
To make your pumpkin come alive,
a candle's all you need.
This Halloween thing is a _____.

She's a spooky creature on Halloween.
Her fur is the color black.
She hisses and howls, meows and purrs,
and arches up her back.
This Halloween animal is a _____.

When kids go out
to trick or treat,
they bring back bags
of this to eat.
This Halloween thing is _____.

Riddle Poem of the Day Scholastic Teaching Resources

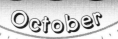

Big Zoo Animals

Its skin is wrinkly.
It's got a trunk.
But not a trunk that's full of junk.
It sprays out water
so don't get in front
of any kind of _____.

She needs her long neck
to eat from trees.
She's covered with spots
but pretty please,
don't ever laugh
at a _____.

It's a furry ape—
the biggest one of all.
It beats its chest and stands up tall.
Don't give your cone—
mint or vanilla—
to any kind of zoo _____.

On the front of its head
it has a horn
just like a beautiful unicorn.
But don't get near or make a fuss
when you go to see the _____.

His *rrroar* is loud.
His *rrroar* is long.
He looks like my cat
but he's big and strong.
I hope it's not me
he seems to be eye-in'
because he's a big ferocious _____.

Write Your Own Riddle:
Letters

There are 26 letters in the ABCs.
Choose one letter from A to Z:
_____ is a little word
(Fill in a short word.)
that starts with this letter.
_____ is a big word
(Fill in a long word.)
and it's even better.
Which letter? _____

Thanksgiving

On Thanksgiving day,
no matter the weather,
the people you love
all gather together . . .
as a f_____.

When you give thanks
for your family and meal
and a place to live,
it makes you feel . . .
so th_____ful.

It's covered with feathers—it's a bird.
"*Gobble, gobble*" it seems to say.
On many tables it's the centerpiece
of a giant feast on Thanksgiving day.
It's a t_____.

They all wore beautiful clothing
and brought fresh corn to eat.
On the very first Thanksgiving,
the pilgrims had a feast
. . . with the I_____.

Space

I'm up in the sky
on a clear, bright night.
I twinkle. I wink.
I'm a sparkly light.
I'm a _____.

We circle the sun.
We are nine in all.
Earth is one, and Mars is one.
We're each shaped like a ball.
We're the _____.

When the sun goes to sleep,
it's my turn to be bright.
I change a little every day.
I'm a giant nightlight.
I'm the _____.

I blast off—*whoosh*
at a very fast pace.
The astronauts ride me
through outer space.
I'm a _____.

Which Dinosaur?

What made this dinosaur great
is a back with pointy plates.
It was much bigger than a bus.
It was a st_____.

It had a pair of horns.
and a collar when it was born.
If you saw it, you wouldn't stop
to pat a big tr_____.

It had a ferocious head and jaw.
On meat, it liked to chop and gnaw.
If you run across it, clear the decks.
It's known as t_____ _____.

If you lined up the dinosaurs all at once,
The biggest was heavy as 20 elephants.
For "massive," it's near the top of the list.
This dinosaur's called a brach_____.

Transportation

I float in the water
with fishes and whales.
The wind helps me move
by pushing my sails.
What am I? _____

With two metal wings,
I fly in the sky.
I soar above clouds
ever so high.
What am I? _____

My wheels roll
on two long tracks.
Chugga-chug-chug.
Clackity-clack.
What am I? _____

I carry loads like logs or fruit
to places near and far.
I'm wide. I'm long. I'm pick-up size.
You pass me in your car.
What am I? _____

Kids can ride me—
here's the deal.
You push the pedals
to turn my two wheels.
What am I? _____

Write Your Own Riddle:
Numbers

I'm less than one hundred,
and I'll always be.

Between _____ and _____
(Fill in the numbers that come just before and just after your mystery number.)

is where to find me.

What number am I? _____

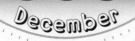

Winter Nappers

I go very deep
into a cave to sleep
until birds in the spring
begin to chirp and cheep.
The cave is my lair.
I am a _____.

I sleep upside-down.
I hang by my feet.
To me a dark cave
is pretty neat.
I'm like a circus acrobat.
You guessed it. I'm a little _____.

I sleep in a hole
in the tall maple tree.
I snack on the nuts
that are underneath me.
Over my face,
my bushy tail curls
because I am a little _____.

In winter
I don't croak or hop.
In a muddy bed
is where I stop,
to sleep at the bottom
of a pond or a bog
because I am a little _____.

Riddle Poem of the Day Scholastic Teaching Resources

Which Coin?

Its color is silver.
It's bigger than a dime.
It's smaller than a quarter
every single time.
Which coin? _____

It's found in people's pockets
all over town.
It's the only coin
that's colored brown.
Which coin? _____

It's the smallest of the coins.
It's silvery and thin.
If you have two bright nickels,
you can trade them in.
Which coin? _____

To make a dollar, you need four—
not one less and not one more.
Each state has a different one.
Are you collecting them for fun?
Which coin? _____

Inventions

Folks talk on me to all their friends,
at home or far away.
In pockets or purses, I *ring, ring, ring,*
as people go on their way.
Which invention am I? _____ _____

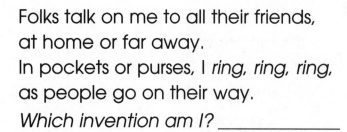

Open my door, put in a pizza,
press a button or two.
I cook your food so quickly.
In seconds, it's ready for you.
Which invention am I? _____

I was invented long ago.
I roll all over town.
I'm part of cars and trucks and bikes.
I'm spinning round and round.

Which invention am I? _____

When I am on,
my screen lights up.
I'm good for e-mail
and playing games.
I even have a little mouse.
Now go ahead and guess my name.
Which invention am I? _____

Your Body

Whenever you're thinking,
you're using this part—
When you read, do science,
math or art.
It's like a computer
inside of you.
It's in your head—
now use the clues!
Which part of your body? _____

There's a pump
inside your body
tha-thump, tha-thump, tha-thump.
You feel it beating extra hard
when you run or swim or jump.
Which part of your body? _____

Take in a great big
breath of air.
Then let it all come out.
This part of your body
that lets you breathe,
you couldn't do without.
Which part of your body? _____

You're filled with 206 of these.
Together they're known as your skeleton.
They run from the top of your head to your toes.
These things are inside everyone.
Which part of your body? _____

This part of your body
digests what you eat,
from bread and potatoes
to chicken and treats.
Which part of your body? _____

Write Your Own Riddle:
Whose Birthday?

This boy/girl has a birthday

in _____ every year.
   (Fill in month.)

His/her initials are _____ _____.
Let's give him/her a great big cheer!

It's _____.

It's _____.

Hooray for _____!

Patterns

Giraffes have splotches.
Cheetahs have spots.
Leopards are known
for their beautiful dots.
Zebras have a pattern
of a different type.
Zebras are covered
with black and white _____.

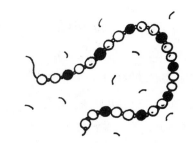

I lined up my marbles
and counted by twos.
I counted again and again.
I always got the same amount:
2, 4, 6, 8, _____.

Here is how I string my beads:
red, blue
red, red, blue
red, blue
red, red, blue.
Come and help me.
What comes next?
Tell me what you would do.

_____

_____

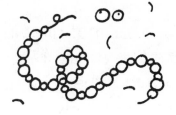

The special pattern
ABCABCABC
is the same as the pattern
fly-slug-bee-fly-slug-bee-fly-slug-bee
and the same as the pattern
1 2 3 ___ ___ ___ ___ ___ ___.

Cold Weather Animals

My tummy is white.
My wings are black.
I'm a bird who doesn't
cheep or *quack*.
I swim in icy water.
I always dive right in
'cause I'm a cute little p_____.

I'm known for my beautiful thick, white fur.
The water I swim in would make you say, "brrr."
I'm found in the Arctic—not everywhere.
I am called a p_____ b_____.

We have tusks that are long.
Flippers move us along.
The name that they call us?
You guessed it! *It's w_____.*

I catch lots of fish with my big strong claws.
I have four furry giant paws.
Stay away and please beware,
because I am a g_____ b_____.

Riddle Poem of the Day Scholastic Teaching Resources

Famous People

He led big peaceful marches.
That was his way to "fight."
His dream was that African Americans
would one day have their rights.
Who is he? _____

This woman wouldn't leave her seat
to sit at the back of the bus.
That day went down in history.
She's a hero to all of us.
Who is she? _____

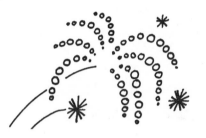

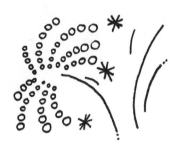

People vote for president
throughout the U.S.A.
_____ 's the name
of the president
who leads the country today.
Who is she/he? _____

There are 50 stars on the flag today
Count them up, wherever you are!
But the woman who sewed
the very first flag
only sewed on 15 stars.
Who is she? _____

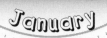

Winter Things

I'm always wearing white.
I have a carrot nose.
When the sun comes out to play,
I melt down to my toes.
What am I? _____

I love to carry you on my back
as I'm sliding down snowy hills.
You yell and scream over all the bumps
'cause riding on me is such a thrill!
What am I? _____

In wintertime, the birds come by
and nibble up my seeds.
I look like a teeny tiny house.
I give birds what they need.
What am I? _____ _____

Riddle Poem of the Day Scholastic Teaching Resources

Each of us is different,
but we like to fall together.
We look like lace or little stars.
We're part of winter weather.
What are we? _____

I make you sniffle and snuffle.
I make you say, "Achoo."
You use a lot of tissues
when I come to visit you.
What am I? _____

Write Your Own Riddle:
Which Month?

It starts with a/an _____.
                    (Fill in a letter.)

It's part of the _____.
                (Fill in *fall, winter, spring,* or *summer.*)

It's the _____ month of the year.
    (Fill in *first, second,* and so on . . . .)

It's known for having _____.
            (Fill in holiday, tradition, or type of weather.)

When it's _____, this month is near.
    (Fill in the month that comes before.)

Habitats

Let's go on safari,
where the grass is wavy and tall.
Zebra, bison, lions too—
this prairie has them all!
Where are we? gr _____

The sand goes on and on.
Bring lots of water to drink.
Be careful, that cactus is very sharp.
And that's a rattlesnake, I think!
Where are we? d _____

Grab your snowshoes and bundle up—
like the polar bear with thick white fur.
That reindeer and that snow white hare
belong in the cold—*BRRR!*
Where are we? A _____

See the animals in the canopy
and all the way down to the forest floor.
See the sloth? Hear the macaw?
That's a jaguar print, I'm pretty sure!
Where are we? r _____ _____

Our Leaders, Our Country

 They say he cut down dad's cherry tree,
but then had to confess.
He became the very first president
of our country—the U.S.
Guess who? _____ _____

His face is on the five-dollar bill
and the coin that says "one cent."
He began to help to free the slaves.
He was our 16th President.
Guess who? _____ _____

 This statue in New York
has a torch in her right hand.
She stands for people's freedom
all across the land.
Guess what? _____

It has a star for every state.
Its colors—red white blue
It waves in every classroom
and at the White House, too.
Guess what? _____

100th Day of School and Other Math Riddles

We folded 50 paper cranes
and hung them in the room.
20 were red and 10 were green
and the rest of them were blue.
How many were blue? _____

Five little sparrows
are eating lunch.
Three more come
to munch and crunch.
Two fly away to tell their friends.
How many birds left in the end? _____

Mel the farmer
wants 100 billy goats.
Today her farm has 60
all wearing shaggy coats.
How many goats to go? _____

5, 10, 15, 20
Valentines! I've got plenty.
The one for you is white and red.
Keep on counting—go ahead.
5, 10, 15, 20, ____, ____, ____, ____, ____, ____, ____,

_____, _____, _____, _____, _____, _____, _____, _____, _____.

Community Helpers

I spy with my little eye
someone with a great big sack.
I hope there's a package or letter for me
when she gets to my house with her big blue pack.
I spy a _____.

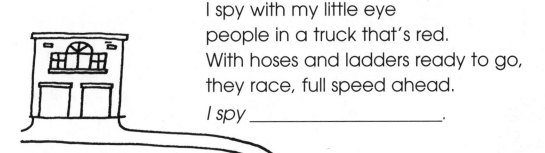

I spy with my little eye
people in a truck that's red.
With hoses and ladders ready to go,
they race, full speed ahead.
I spy _____.

I spy with my little eye
someone reading a story out loud.
All around are shelves of books.
I take some home 'cause it's allowed!
I spy a _____.

I spy with my little eye
someone checking the beat of my heart.
She looks in my mouth to check my throat.
Then she writes things down on her little chart.
I spy a _____.

I spy with my little eye
someone who teaches important things.
That person's at the classroom door
every time the first bell rings.
Who do I spy? _____

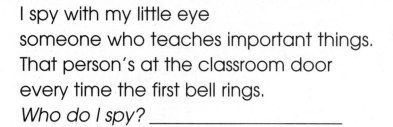

I spy with my little eye
a car with a light that spins around.
The person inside keeps everyone safe
and helps out people all over town.
Who do I spy? _____

Write Your Own Riddle:
A Valentine

Can you name this friend of mine?
I want to give her/him a Valentine.
This friend's wearing _____ and _____ today.
        (Fill in a color.)   (Fill in another color.)
and her/his hair is _____ every day.
    (Fill in a color or a describing word like *curly*.)

Spring Things

You can tell we're back
when you hear us sing.
We build our nests
as soon as it's spring.
Who's back? _____

For now we're buds
but soon we'll be open.
We'll soak up some water—
at least that's what we're hopin'.
What spring things are we? _____

At one end of a rainbow
is where I hide my gold.
I'm tricky,
I wear green,
and I'm very, very old.
What spring thing am I? _____

We cannot fly all by ourselves.
We need some windy weather.
You hold us by our long, white strings.
We swoop and soar together.
What spring things are we? _____

Fruits and Vegetables

Raw or cooked
or part of soup,
There are many ways to prepare it.
It's orange with wild green leaves on top.
It's a crunchy, munchy _____.

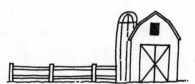

They never grow alone.
They like having company.
They're green and roll around your plate.
Gee, what could they be? _____.

They always grow in bunches.
They're round or oval in shape.
They're purple or red or green.
They're big fat juicy _____.

Green on the outside,
pink inside.
This fruit is so sweet smellin'.
In summertime, they're always sellin'
great big, ripened _____.

What My Garden Needs

If my garden doesn't have it,
then everything gets dry.
I can bring it in a hose,
or it comes down from the sky.
What does my garden need? _____

At first they fit inside my hand.
They're usually very small.
But then they grow into plants—
bushy, bright, or tall.
What does my garden need? _____

It keeps my garden warm all day.
It makes the leaves look green and bright.
It shines down on my growing plants
and only goes away at night.
What does my garden need? _____

It's a soft, dark home for roots to grow.
It's where I plant my seeds.
I keep it nice and wet.
I dig out all its weeds.
What does my garden need? _____

Animals Use Their Senses

Scraps from the trash
at the beach are yummy!
But picnic food is
great in my tummy!
What sense is the seagull using? _____

There's a laughing hyena,
a roaring lion,
a jungle bird
that sounds like it's cryin'.
What sense is the elephant using? _____

This rock's so smooth
against my scales.
It's warmed up by the sunny rays.
And when I've sunbathed long enough,
the river's cool for the rest of the day.
What sense is the alligator using? _____

Riddle Poem of the Day Scholastic Teaching Resources

There goes a school of butterfly fish
all yellow and shiny black.
There goes a silly clown fish
with polka dots on its back.
What sense is the sea turtle using? _____

My nose tells me
a bone's buried here
and that my owner
is pretty near.
What sense is the dog using? _____

Write Your Own Riddle:
What Time Is It?

The big hand's on the _____.
                        (Fill in the numeral that tells the hour.)

The little hand's on the _____.
                        (Fill in the numeral that tells the minutes.)

It's time to _____, yessiree.
            (Fill in something you do at this time.)

So what time could it be?

It's _____.

On the Farm

We pick it up with pitchforks
as the horses all cry *neigh.*
We feed the horses every day
with the farm-grown _____ .

It's home to the cows and horses.
It's a building on the farm.
It's where the farm cats chase the mice.
It is the big red _____ .

The dairy farmer sells his goods
At a stand near a green hill
he's got yummy yellow butter for sale
and jugs of fresh white _____ .

The rooster wakes us up
as soon as the day is new.
He's everyone's alarm clock,
saying, " _____ .*"*

Helping the Earth

Let's make sure the sky
is always clean and blue.
The animals breathe it day and night
and guess what? So do you!
What should we keep clean? a_____

Be sure you save
your plastic and cans.
We want to help,
so that's our plan.
What can you do to help the planet? r_____

Whenever you're near the oceans,
the rivers, and the streams,
be sure to pick up all your trash
to keep our planet clean.
What should we keep clean? w_____

If you want to help the earth
recycle the paper you use.
Think of the beautiful things you'll save.
They're a resource we don't want to lose.
What don't we want to lose? t_____

In the Rain Forest

A wild cat's prowling in the night,
with brownish-yellow fur.
It's covered all in blackish spots.
When it's angry it says *GRRR*.
You won't need to look very far
before seeing a wild _____.

A bird is flitting through the trees.
Its feathers are paint-box bright.
With a yellow beak so large,
this bird is quite a sight.
Now take a guess if you can.
This creature is a _____.

A lizard is crawling on the forest floor.
Its skin is scaly green.
It looks like a little dinosaur.
When still, it can hardly be seen.
So guess its name, if you wanna.
It's the strange, but cute _____.

A mammal is swinging through the trees.
It's noisy when it howls and hoots.
It hangs by its legs and even its tail
and gobbles leaves and forest fruits.
This animal is very spunky.
And it is called a howler _____.

Who's Inside the Egg?

I'm waiting inside
curled up in a ball.
I have a forked tongue
and no legs at all.
Who's inside the egg? _____

I'm waiting inside
all fuzzy and yellow.
I have feathers and wings.
I'm a cute little fellow.
Who's inside the egg? _____

I'm waiting inside
with a shell on my back.
I may hide and be shy
when my soft egg cracks.
Who's inside the egg? _____

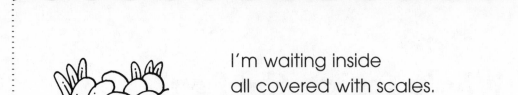

I'm waiting inside
all covered with scales.
I have very big jaws
and a long, strong tail.
Who's inside the egg? _____

I'm waiting inside
way up high in a nest.
When I'm hatched and I'm hungry,
I like worms the best.
Who's inside the egg? _____

Write Your Own Riddle:
Clothing and Weather

I put on my _____.
            (Fill in a type of clothing.)

I put on my _____.
            (Fill in a type of clothing.)

'Cause the weather is _____.
            (Fill in *cool, cold, warm,* or *hot*.)

And that's a very good reason . . .

I know! I know! _____ is the season.

Baby Animals

I hear with my little ear
a *baaa, baaa, baaa.*
This baby's too young for its wool to be sheared
it's calling to its ma.
Which baby animal is it? _____

I hear with my little ear
a soft *neigh, neigh.*
When this baby grows up big and strong,
it will trot and gallop all day.
Which baby animal is it? _____

I hear with my little ear
an *oink, oink* sound.
This baby's pink with a curly tail.
In the mud it rolls around.
Which baby animal is it? _____

I hear with my little ear
a *quack, quack, quack.*
This baby paddles with big webbed feet
and water rolls off its back.
Which baby animal is it? _____

Famous Bugs

I'm famous for rolling in a ball
when someone touches me.
But I'd go crawling all about
if you'd just let me be!
Which famous bug am I? _____ _____

I'm famous for spinning gorgeous webs
all over the bushes and trees.
I think eight legs are beautiful,
but some of you disagree.
Which famous bug am I? _____

I'm famous for my polka dots
and for my bright red shell.
When I land on you and crawl around,
you think it's pretty swell.
Which famous bug am I? _____

I'm famous for blinking on and off
on long, hot summer nights.
You try to catch me in your jar
because of my flickering light.
Which famous bug am I? _____

Riddle Poem of the Day Scholastic Teaching Resources

Life Cycles

Out of a little tiny egg
comes a caterpillar in the spring.
Then out from inside its chrysalis
comes a b_____ with fragile wings.

It starts as an egg,
goes from chick to h_____.
Then it clucks and it sits on
brown eggs again.

The s_____ starts as a little seed.
It grows roots, leaves, and stem.
Then you pick the seeds from its giant flower,
and roast and munch on them.

It starts as an egg
and then becomes
a tadpole with a tail.
And once it's gotten all four legs,
It's a hoppity _____, never fail.

Families: Timmy's Family

Timmy calls his parents
his __ __ __ and his __ __ __
They love him and care for him
and that makes Timmy glad.

Timmy's got lots of __ __ __ __ __ __ __
   and __ __ __ __ __ __ __ __
of all different ages.
And in the family scrapbooks
their photos fill the pages.

Timmy's mother has a mother.
Her name is G __ __ __ __ __ __ Sue.
She always brings a treat for him
'cause that's what she likes to do.

Lots of Timmy's family
come over for the holidays.
And all his dozens of c __ __ __ __ __ __
just run around and play.

Timmy's dad has an older sister.
Lily is her name.
A __ __ __ Lily looks like Timmy's dad
and they always laugh the same.

Timmy's mother's brother
is his cool U __ __ __ __ Lee.
He plays lots of sports
and tells lots of jokes.
He's always fun to see.

Write Your Own Riddle:
Addition

_____ little chimps
(Fill in a number.)
were swinging in a tree.

_____ more came
(Fill in a number.)
and hung by their knees.

That's _____ chimps in all,
as silly as can be—
swinging and hanging
from the jungle tree.

Small Animals

I love to eat cheese.
I'm not so strong.
I squeak, squeak, squeak
and my tail is long.
Which small animal am I? m_____

Most birds are small
but I am tiny.
I'm teeny as can be.
I zip around.
My wings beat fast.
They're pretty hard to see.
Which small animal am I? h_____

I look like a miniature alligator.
I'm often green or brown.
You'll find me climbing in the trees
or darting on the ground.
Which small animal am I? i_____

Croak, croak.
I sound like a frog.
I look like a frog looks, too.
I'm brown with a very warty back
and a tongue that sticks like glue.
Which small animal am I? t_____

Ocean Animals

You're swimming in the ocean
when a creature says "hello."
Its eight legs dance and float around.
But it's scared and has to go.
Guess who? _____

You're walking by the ocean
when a creature says "hello."
Its many arms cling to the rocks
It's a star but doesn't glow.
Guess who? _____

You're walking by the ocean
when a creature says "hello."
You see its spout and giant tail
and then it dives below.
Guess who? _____

You're swimming in the ocean
when a creature says "hello."
It squeals and gives a friendly smile.
Then waves its fins and goes.
Guess who? _____

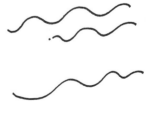

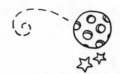

Which Sport?

Dribble and pass. Dribble and pass.
Kick a black and white ball.
Boot it straight into the goal.
Watch for mud—don't fall!
Which sport? _____

A cartwheel here.
A back flip there.
You're flipping
and turning
in the air!
Which sport? _____

Dribble, dribble.
Shoot the ball.
Watch it soaring high.
If it missed the basket,
give it another try!
Which sport? _____

You smack the ball.
You run, run, run.
You touch every base
for your first homerun!
Which sport? _____

Dive from the side.
Hold your breath.
The water is very cool.
Arms turn, legs kick
in the lovely light-blue pool.
Which sport? _____

Summer Things

You hear a *CRASH*.
You hear a *BOOM*,
whenever I'm nearby.
You see a long, white zigzag
flash-flashing in the sky.
What summer thing am I? _____

I'm barbecues.
I'm watermelon.
I'm crunchy potato chips.
I'm eating on the summer grass.
I'm ants and doggy yips.
What summer thing am I? _____

I'm bare feet on the hot, hot sand.
I'm seagulls flying by.
I'm waves and boats
and suntan lotion.
I'm sunshine in the sky.
What summer thing am I? _____

I'm perfect for
hot summer days
in bathing suits or clothes.
You run through me
and scream and yell.
My water's from the hose.
What summer thing am I? _____

I can be purple
or yellow or red.
I'm very cold and sweet.
You love to lick me in summertime.
I'm a drippy, icy treat.
What summer thing am I? _____

Write Your Own Riddle:
Subtraction

_____ little hamsters spinning round and round.
(Fill in a number.)
The wheels make such a squeaky sound.
They all feel dizzy

and _____ fall down.
(Fill in a lower number.)
How many hamsters left spinning around? _____

Riddle Poem of the Day Scholastic Teaching Resources

SEPTEMBER

What's in the Classroom?, page 11
pencil
paper
books
scissors

Feelings, page 12
angry/mad
sad
happy
scared/afraid

Which School Subject?, page 13
math
reading
art
science

Which Day of the Week?, page 14
Monday
Friday
Thursday
Wednesday
Tuesday

Write Your Own Riddle:
Guess Which Student, page 15
Answers will vary.

OCTOBER

Guess My Shape, page 16
circle
triangle
square
rectangle

Fall Things, page 17
wind
apples
pumpkins
leaves

Halloween, page 18
bat
jack-o-lantern
cat
candy

Big Zoo Animals, page 19
elephant
giraffe
gorilla
rhinoceros
lion

Write Your Own Riddle:
Letters, page 20
Answers will vary.

NOVEMBER

Thanksgiving, page 21
family
thankful
turkey
Indians

Space, page 22
star
planets
moon
spaceship/rocket ship

Which Dinosaur?, page 23
stegosaurus
triceratops
tyrannosaurus rex
brachiosaurus

Transportation, page 24
boat/sailboat
airplane
train
truck
bicycle
Write Your Own Riddle:
Numbers, page 25
Answers will vary.

DECEMBER

Winter Nappers, page 26
bear
bat
squirrel
frog

Which Coin?, page 27
nickel
penny
dime
quarter

Inventions, page 28
cell phone
microwave
wheel
computer

Your Body, page 29
brain
heart
lungs
bones
stomach
Write Your Own Riddle:
Whose Birthday?, page 30
Answers will vary.

JANUARY

Patterns, page 31
stripes
10
red, blue / red, red, blue
123123

Cold Weather Animals, page 32
penguin
polar bear
walrus
grizzly bear

Famous People, page 33
Dr. Martin Luther King, Jr.
Rosa Parks
name of current President of the
United States
Betsy Ross

Winter Things, page 34
snowman
sled/sleigh
bird feeder
snowflakes
a cold/the flu
Write Your Own Riddle:
Which Month?, page 35
Answers will vary.

FEBRUARY

Habitats, page 36
grasslands
desert
Arctic
rain forest

Our Leaders, Our Country, page 37
George Washington
Abraham Lincoln
Statue of Liberty
U.S. flag

100th Day of School and Other Math Riddles, page 38
20
6
40
25, 30, 35, 40, 45, 50, 55, 60, 65, 70,
75, 80, 85, 90, 95, 100

Community Helpers, page 39
mail carrier, postal carrier
firefighters
librarian
doctor
teacher
police officer

Write Your Own Riddle:
A Valentine, page 40
Answers will vary.

MARCH

Spring Things, page 41
birds
flowers
leprechaun
kites

Fruits and Vegetables, page 42
carrot
peas
grapes
watermelon

What My Garden Needs, page 43
water
seeds
sun
soil/dirt

Animals Use Their Senses, page 44
taste
hearing
touch
sight
smell

Write Your Own Riddle:
What Time Is It?, page 45
Answers will vary.

APRIL

On the Farm, page 46
hay
barn
milk
cock-a-doodle-doo

Helping the Earth, page 47
air
recycle
water
trees

In the Rain Forest, page 48
jaguar
toucan
iguana
monkey

Who's Inside the Egg?, page 49
snake
chick
turtle

alligator
bird

Write Your Own Riddle:
Clothing and Weather, page 50
Answers will vary.

MAY

Baby Animals, page 51
baby sheep/lamb
baby horse/colt
baby pig/piglet
baby duck/duckling

Famous Bugs, page 52
roly poly/potato bug
spider
ladybug
firefly

Life Cycles, page 53
butterfly
hen
sunflower
frog

Families: Timmy's Family, page 54
mom and dad
sisters and brothers
Grandma
cousins
Aunt
Uncle

Write Your Own Riddle:
Addition, page 55
Answers will vary.

JUNE

Small Animals, page 56
mouse
hummingbird
lizard (or salamander)
toad

Ocean Animals, page 57
octopus
starfish
whale
dolphin/porpoise

Which Sport?, page 58
soccer
basketball
gymnastics
baseball
swimming

Summer Things, page 59
lightning
picnic
beach/ocean/shore
sprinkler
Popsicle

Write Your Own Riddle:
Subtraction,
page 60
Answers will vary.